W9-BYH-096

OSPREYS

DOUG WECHSLER

THE ACADEMY OF NATURAL SCIENCES

The Rosen Publishing Group's
PowerKids Press™
New York

For Dave, MarySue, Nick, and Veronica.
Thanks to Alan Poole, whose writings have been an important resource, for comments on the manuscript.

About the Author
Wildlife biologist, ornithologist, and photographer Doug Wechsler has studied birds, snakes, frogs, and other wildlife around the world. Doug Wechsler works at The Academy of Natural Sciences of Philadelphia, a natural history museum. As part of his job, he travels to rain forests and remote parts of the world to take pictures of birds. He has taken part in expeditions to Ecuador, the Philippines, Borneo, Cuba, Cameroon, and many other countries.

Published in 2001 by The Rosen Publishing Group, Inc.
29 East 21st Street, New York, NY 10010

Copyright © 2001 by The Rosen Publishing Group, Inc.

All rights reserved. No part of this book may be reproduced in any form without permission in writing from the publisher, except by a reviewer.

First Edition

Book Design: Michael de Guzman

Photo Credits: Doug Wechsler portrait by Bruce Hallett; p. 4 © J.H. Dick/VIREO; p. 7 © A. & S. Carey/VIREO; p. 8 © A. & S. Carey/VIREO; p. 11 © T. J. Ulrich/VIREO; p. 12 © A. & S. Carey/VIREO; p. 12 © F. Truslow/VIREO; p. 15 © F. Truslow/VIREO; p. 16 © A. & E. Morris/VIREO; p. 19 © Doug Wechsler; p. 20 © J. Heidecker/VIREO; p. 22 © J. Heidecker/VIREO. All photographs from VIREO (Visual Resources for Ornithology), The Academy of Natural Sciences' worldwide collection of bird photographs.

Wechsler, Doug.
    Ospreys / Doug Wechsler.
      p. cm— (The really wild life of birds of prey)
    Summary: Describes the appearance, food, nests, migration, and other behavioral characteristics of the osprey, also known as the fishhawk.
    ISBN 0-8239-5597-4 (lib. bdg. : alk. paper)
    1. Osprey—Juvenile literature. [1. Osprey.] I. Title.
QL696.F36 W43 2000

99-059410

Manufactured in the United States of America

CONTENTS

A BIRD OF THE WORLD

A brown and white bird with crooked wings sails over the marsh. It whistles a loud "eee-eee-eee-eee." The sound is familiar to fishermen around the world. It is the call of the osprey. The osprey is a large **raptor** related to hawks and eagles. Ospreys live on every **continent** except Antarctica.

Ospreys are sometimes known as fish hawks. This name fits them well. They make their living fishing. Ospreys are larger than red-tailed hawks and smaller than bald eagles. From wing tip to wing tip they measure about 5 1/2 feet (1.7 m).

An osprey is brown on top and white on the bottom. It has a white head with a wide dark brown band across the eye.

FISH, FISH, FISH

Ospreys eat fish for breakfast and fish for lunch. They even eat fish for dinner. An osprey eats almost nothing but fish! Ospreys feed on fish that swim near the surface of the water where they can catch them. Ospreys do not bother with fish that are too small or too large. Their favorite size of fish is about half a pound (227 g).

Ospreys are fish eaters. They dive feet first into the water when catching fish.

THE FISHING MACHINE

Ospreys are fish-eating **specialists**. A specialist is an animal that lives in only one kind of environment or eats only one kind of food. An osprey's whole body is made for catching and eating fish. Its feet have rough bumps to help the osprey hold onto its slimy **prey**. An osprey's feathers are very oily to keep them from soaking up water. The osprey can even close its **nostrils** to keep water out as it splashes below the surface of water.

An osprey's feet have rough bumps to help it hold onto slippery fish.

TAKING THE PLUNGE

It is exciting to watch ospreys hunt. They fly over shallow water looking for fish. If they find a good fishing spot, they stop in midair and **hover**. When an osprey spots its prey, it folds its wings and dives, shooting headfirst toward the water. Just an instant before the osprey hits, it brings its legs forward and plunges into the water. The osprey disappears in the splashing water for a moment as it grasps the fish, then takes off. With the fish in its **talons**, the osprey rises in the air and shakes the water off its feathers.

After it has a fish in its talons, an osprey rises and shakes the water from its oily feathers.

DOUG SAYS

AN OSPREY CAN CLOSE ITS TALONS FASTER THAN YOU CAN BLINK AN EYE.

DOUG SAYS

A PAIR OF OSPREYS MAY MAKE MORE THAN 100 TRIPS TO THE NEST WHEN THEY ARE BUILDING IT.

A NEST YOU CANNOT MISS

Unlike most birds, an osprey does not try to hide its nest. Instead it chooses a place in the open. This place can be on top of a dead tree. It can also be a cliff or a special man-made platform built for ospreys. Having a nest in the open helps an osprey see other ospreys. It even allows an osprey to see its enemies, like eagles, owls, and raccoons. Having a nest in the open makes it easy for this big-winged bird to fly in and out of its home.

Both parents build the nest. They use sticks, seaweed, and even garbage. Even after they lay the eggs, the ospreys bring more sticks from time to time.

Ospreys use their nest year after year so the nest just keeps getting bigger.

HOMEBODIES

In the spring and summer, ospreys spend most of their time near the nest. It takes almost six weeks to **incubate** the eggs. The female usually sits on the eggs at night, but during the day the male helps out. As the young are growing up, the father goes fishing and the mother feeds the catch to the little ones. After a few weeks, the **nestlings** can tear the fish apart by themselves. When they are eight weeks old, the young ospreys are finally ready to **fledge**, or fly, from the nest.

The mother osprey feeds the babies until they are about three weeks old. After that, the nestlings can tear the fish themselves.

DOUG SAYS

THE OLDEST KNOWN OSPREY LIVED TO BE 31 YEARS OLD.

FRIENDLY NEIGHBORS

Unlike most raptors, ospreys sometimes live in **colonies**. If there are plenty of fish, ospreys will nest within a few hundred feet (a couple hundred meters) of one another. Sitting on its nest tree, a male osprey watches a neighbor fly home with a fish. Does he learn from his neighbor where the fish are today? We do not know, but off he goes, perhaps in search of a meal.

The male osprey fishes for food while the female osprey stays in the nest with the young.

HOW TO CATCH AN OSPREY

Did you ever wonder how a **scientist** catches an osprey to study it? The easiest way is to use a trap called a noose carpet. A noose carpet is a roof of wire mesh with many little knots tied to it. The roof fits nicely on top of the nest. The knots, or nooses, are made with fishing line and have an open loop. When the parents leave, the scientist quickly ties the noose carpet over the nest. When the osprey returns, its feet end up inside the loops. As it moves, the knots tighten around the feet. The scientist quickly climbs up a ladder and holds the osprey by the legs to remove the knots. The noose carpet does not hurt the osprey.

Scientists use a noose carpet to catch an osprey so they can study it. ▶

DOUG SAYS

UNLIKE MOST RAPTORS, OSPREYS ARE NOT AFRAID TO NEST NEAR PEOPLE.

OSPREYS LIVE NEAR PEOPLE

Most raptors are shy and stay away from people. Ospreys, though, have **adapted** to living near us. As long as they have a good supply of their favorite fish, they usually find a way to get along with people. Sometimes ospreys nest next to bridges with heavy traffic. They also nest next to boat docks, on the tops of **buoys**, and even on power poles. Cars and boats do not bother them, but they will usually fly away if someone walks close to their nest. People who like ospreys have built nest platforms for them.

Ospreys usually build their nests in the tops of trees. Sometimes they will build their nests on power poles or man-made platforms.

THE LONG MIGRATION

When fall comes, ospreys in the north **migrate** to tropical climates. They leave cold areas long before the lakes and rivers freeze over. They cannot catch fish below the ice. Ospreys living in warmer places, such as the state of Florida, do not need to leave.

Ospreys are strong fliers. They cross deserts and oceans on their migratory flights. It is fun to watch them fly by because they often carry a fish with them. Ospreys always carry the fish with its head pointing forward. They will eat the fish along the way during the long journey. After it reaches Florida, the osprey flies across the Caribbean Sea to South America. Then in March it returns home.

GLOSSARY

adapted (uh-DAPT-ed) To have changed to fit new conditions.

buoys (boo-EEZ) Anchored objects floating on the water to warn against hidden rocks or to show the safe part of a waterway.

colonies (KAHL-ah-neez) Groups living and interacting together.

continent (KON-tin-ent) One of the seven great masses of land on earth.

fledge (FLEDJ) To fly from the nest for the first time.

hover (HUV-er) To fly in place in the air.

incubate (IN-kyoo-bayt) To keep eggs warm, usually at body temperature.

migrate (MY-grayt) To regularly move to a faraway place to spend the season.

nestlings (NEST-lingz) Young birds that are still in the nest.

nostrils (NOS-trelz) The openings to the nose. Birds (and other animals) breathe through their nostrils.

prey (PRAY) Animals that are food for other animals.

raptor (RAP-ter) A sharp-clawed bird that hunts other animals.

scientist (SY-en-tist) A person who studies the way things are and act in the world and universe.

specialists (SPESH-uhl-ists) Animals that eat only one kind of food, or live in only one kind of place.

talons (TA-luns) Sharp, curved claws on a bird of prey.

INDEX

WEB SITES

To learn more about ospreys, check out these Web sites:

http://www.raptor.cvm.umn.edu/
http://www.hawkmountain.org/
http://www.id.blm.gov/bopnca/index.html
http://acnatsci.org/vireo (Readers can order a raptor slide set.)

24

W9-BOO-551

Peter's Painting

BY **SALLY MOSS**

ILLUSTRATED BY **MEREDITH THOMAS**

BEDFORD HILLS FREE LIBRARY
BEDFORD HILLS NY

Peter painted a bird.

He painted it over and over.

And the more Peter painted,

the more his bird flew.

Peter's bird flew
and flew and flew.

Peter painted a snake.

He painted it over and over.

And the more Peter painted,

the more his snake slithered.

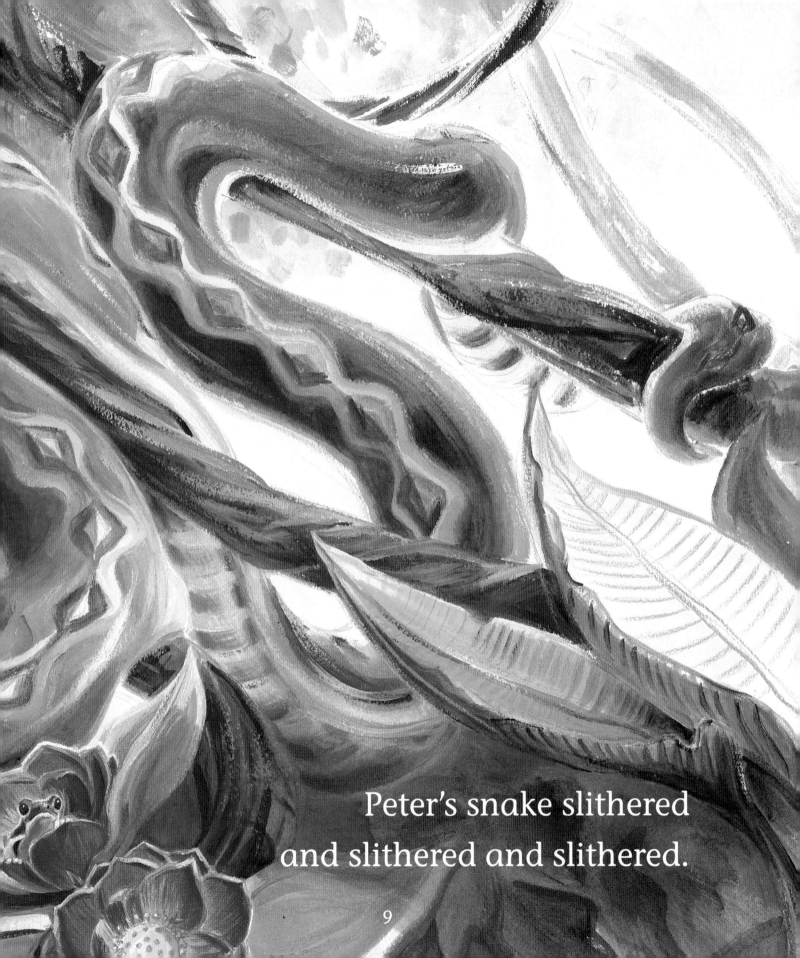

Peter's snake slithered
and slithered and slithered.

Peter painted a fish.

He painted it over and over.

And the more Peter painted,

the more his fish swam.

Peter's fish swam
and swam and swam.

13

Peter painted a star.

He painted it over and over.

And the more Peter painted,

the more his star twinkled.

Peter's star twinkled
and twinkled and twinkled.

BEDFORD HILLS FREE LIBRARY
BEDFORD HILLS NY

Peter painted a door.

He painted it over and over.

18

And the more Peter painted,

the more his door opened.

Peter's door
opened
and
opened
and
opened.

21

And Peter leaped into the world,

into the world he had painted.